Photo by Joan Marcus

A scene from the Playwrights Horizons production of "Sophistry." Set design by Allen

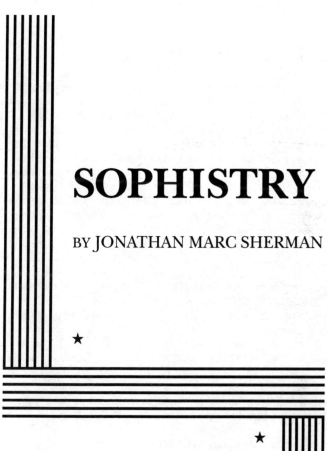

SOPHISTRY

BY JONATHAN MARC SHERMAN

★

★

DRAMATISTS
PLAY SERVICE
INC.

For my dearest Jessica,
no possession implied.

SOPHISTRY received its premiere at Playwrights Horizons (Don Scardino, Artistic Director; Leslie Marcus, Managing Director), in New York City, on October 11, 1993. It was directed by Nicholas Martin; the set design was by Allen Moyer; the costume design was by Michael Krass; the lighting design was by Kenneth Posner; the sound design was by Jeremy Grody and the production stage manager was Christopher Wigle. The cast was as follows:

WHITEY McCOY...Austin Pendleton
WILLY... Steve Zahn
IGOR KONIGSBERG ....Jonathan Marc Sherman
XAVIER (EX) REYNOLDS.................................... Ethan Hawke
ROBIN SMITH..Calista Flockhart
JACK KAHN ....Anthony Rapp
DEBBIE .... Nadia Dajani
QUINTANA MATHESON ....Linda Atkinson

SOPHISTRY received a workshop production at Playwrights Horizons' New Theater Wing, in March, 1993, with the same cast, except for WHITEY McCOY (Dick Latessa), ROBIN SMITH (Katherine Hiler), and CHILD (Scarlett Johansson). The role of the Child was subsequently cut, in spite of Miss Johansson's lovely performance in the role.

"But it was an experience. I will not turn him into an anecdote. How do we fit what happened to us into life without turning it into an anecdote with no teeth and a punch line you'll mouth over and over for years to come .... How do we <u>keep</u> the experience?"

— John Guare, *Six Degrees of Separation*

"You know, if the moment is right, the candles are just right and the drink is just right and the music is just right and <u>you're</u> just right and she's just right, and you lean over and touch her hand, it's <u>magic</u>. If the moment is wrong, it's your clammy hand on the back of her sweaty hand, and it doesn't work."

— Mario Cuomo, *American Heritage interview,* December 1990

CHARACTERS

WHITEY McCOY – 55. Philosophy professor.
WILLY
IGOR KONIGSBERG
XAVIER (EX) REYNOLDS
ROBIN SMITH
JACK KAHN
DEBBIE
QUINTANA MATHESON – 50. College president.

The action of the play takes place from May 1990 to June 1991 in various locations, most of them on the campus of a small New England college.

CHRONOLOGY

ACT ONE, Scenes 1–8, May–June 1990
ACT ONE, Scenes 9–10, December 1990

ACT TWO, Scenes 1–2, March–April 1991
ACT TWO, Scenes 3–8, May–June 1991

SOPHISTRY

ACT ONE

Scene 1

Whitey McCoy is teaching his philosophy class. Willy, Robin, and Debbie sit downstage, with their backs to the audience.

WHITEY.   What is the value of value? Who are we, and what is important to us? To the Sophists, it wasn't important whether or not you were right or wrong. The cleverness of your argument was —
WILLY.   Was this before or after Socrates?
WHITEY.   *Pre*-Socratic. *(Beat.)* The Sophists argued *both* sides of an argument, sharpened their skills, became better, *more* clever, *more* persuasive —
WILLY.   Is this going to be on the test?
WHITEY.   Perhaps. *(Beat.)* Values shifted, the nature of — *(Igor enters with an envelope.)*
IGOR.   Sorry to interrupt.
WHITEY.   What's this?
IGOR.   From President Matheson. She told me to deliver it personally. Pretty important, I guess. *(Igor gives Whitey the envelope.)*
WILLY.   Yo, Igor.
IGOR.   *(Looking out.)* Yo, Willy. What's up?
WILLY.   Nothing.
WHITEY.   *(To Igor.)* Is that all?
IGOR.   Huh?
WHITEY.   Is that all?
IGOR.   Oh, yeah, that'll be all. See ya. Later, Willy.
WILLY.   Bye. *(Igor exits.)*

WHITEY. Shall we … continue?

WILLY. What's in the envelope, Teach?

WHITEY. Something that can *wait. (Beat.)* Now, to return to the Sophists —

WILLY. Will this be on the test?

WHITEY. *Yes.*

Scene 2

Igor reads the school newspaper, Willy keeps himself occupied, Ex tunes his guitar. They are all 20, all guys.

IGOR. They might install one of those automatic cash machines on campus. For magnetic bank cards. We'd be able to withdraw cash without driving into town.

WILLY. Good idea.

EX. *Bad* idea. The administration would monitor the thing. They'd know when drugs were coming onto campus. They'd keep lists of names … Big Brother … waves of people start withdrawing, they know a shipment's arrived. "Lots of people are taking out thirty dollars, the pot has arrived … people are withdrawing a hundred dollars, cocaine, cocaine." The thing would be a private detective without the heart. More technology nobody understands. More disconnection.

WILLY. Come on. It's cool and convenient. Money at your fingertips.

IGOR. Robin wrote an article.

EX. She always gets one in. My girl.

IGOR. How fast can she type?

EX. *Really* fast.

IGOR. You think she'd type my paper?

EX. Probably not.

WILLY. I have to find somebody to type a paper for me. After I find somebody to *write* it. Does anybody have one of those catalogues that sells term papers?

EX. I have a Victoria's Secret catalogue.

WILLY. *(To Igor.)* Hey, what'd Matheson want from Whitey that was so red hot?

IGOR. I couldn't find out. Very hush hush. Top secret and all. Sealed envelope. Closed door.

EX. Maybe they're having an affair. Whitey and Quintana. Imagine that?

WILLY. Imagine Liberace and the Hoover Dam. *(Robin enters. She is 20.)* Hey, Robin.

ROBIN. Ex, can I talk to you for a minute?

EX. We're rehearsing.

ROBIN. Willy and Igor aren't even in the vicinity of their instruments.

EX. Brainstorming. Lyrics. It's a *session.* We can talk at dinner.

ROBIN. I really need —

EX. Honey, it's rehearsal time. Sacred. My music.

ROBIN. *(Beat.)* Dinner. *(Robin exits.)*

WILLY. Bye, Robin. *(Beat.)* Man, what's *that* all about?

EX. I don't know. She's been freaking out lately. Yesterday, she tells me — right when we're in bed together, she's being all *distant,* I ask her what's wrong, she tells me, "It's just that I used to trust your kisses so much more." You believe that? I mean, where does something like that *come* from?

WILLY. I don't know, man. *(Beat.)* You still fucking around with Sharon?

EX. What do *you* think? *(Beat.)* Yeah, of *course* I'm still fucking around with Sharon, but, you know, where does Robin get off saying something like that, "I used to trust your kisses so much more?" Where does she get *off?*

9

Scene 3

Whitey is drinking tea. Ex enters.

EX. Whitey —

WHITEY. Ex, I'm glad you're here, do you want some tea?

EX. Nah.

WHITEY. Are you sure? It's *made.* Chamomile. It *soothes.*

EX. All right, sure.

WHITEY. Good. *(Whitey pours some tea, and Ex takes a sip.)*

EX. So, what's going on?

WHITEY. Something has happened. An *accusation.* I'm going to need you to testify as to my *character.*

EX. Wait, go back. What *kind* of accusation? Who's accusing who?

WHITEY. Somebody's accusing *me.* I'm being accused.

EX. Of what? Why are you being so *odd,* Whitey? What's going on? What are you accused of?

WHITEY. A student — *Jack Kahn* — has accused me of sexually harassing him.

EX. What? Is this —

WHITEY. This is serious. He has accused me of ... well, essentially, of *molesting* him. Of *raping* him.

EX. That kid's a freak. He's on a twenty-four-hour-a-day acid trip. He's taken — the fucking freak's a friggin' frequent *flyer,* he's taken so many trips.

WHITEY. I *know.*

EX. What happened?

WHITEY. Well, he *claims* that I was drunk, that I forced him to remove his clothing, that I threatened his life, that I —

EX. Get out of *town.* This is a sick joke.

WHITEY. He *says* I performed fellatio on him, and that I attempted to make him perform it on me. He *claims* all of this took place during Thanksgiving break, this *rape,* and that he's repressed it all this time, for months, but finally he just *had* to confess what happened, he just *had* to get it all out.

EX.   *(Beat.)* It's not — I mean, he's *sick*, right? None of it is *true*, right?

WHITEY.   Of *course* not.

EX.   I had to ask. I know that. I just — *(Beat.)* What really went on? *Anything? Something* must have triggered him —

WHITEY.   I did see him during Thanksgiving break, *that's* true. He was having trouble with my class and wanted to discuss it. Probably wanted a break, wanted to *weasel* out of doing his work. I was sleeping. I heard the bell ringing. I tried to ignore it. It would not stop. So, I got up, put on my robe, and went to the door. *(Jack Kahn enters. He is 20.)* Jack, what are you doing? Do you know what *time* it is?

JACK.   Yeah, it's three in the morning. I really have to talk to you. It's important. I'm really scared. I'm messed up. I'm totally messed up. Totally scared. Messed up.

WHITEY.   *(To Ex.)* He was clearly high, God knows on what. *(To Jack.)* All right, come inside, you'll freeze to death out there dressed like that. Take off your shoes and place them near the door. I don't want snow and slush tramped all over my floor. *(Jack takes off his shoes.)* Do you want some tea?

JACK.   Do you have something *spicier?* Something I can really *drink?*

WHITEY.   Jack, let's not be too *coy.* What would you like?

JACK.   You have any vodka?

WHITEY.   Any particular *brand?*

JACK.   Umm —

WHITEY.   I'm joking, Jack. I'm joking. *(Whitey pours a shot of vodka, and Jack drinks it.)*

JACK.   That's the trick. That's warm, that *bites.* Another?

WHITEY.   A real drinker, are you? *(Whitey pours a shot, Jack drinks it.)*

JACK.   Another.

WHITEY.   I don't think it's the best of ideas, Jack —

JACK.   Just one more, Whitey, *please.* I really need it, I'm real messed up.

WHITEY.   This is *vodka*, Jack, not water. If you are indeed "messed up," perhaps —

JACK.   Just one more.

WHITEY.   *(Beat.) Reluctantly. (Whitey pours a shot, Jack drinks it.)*

JACK.   Another.

WHITEY.   *Jack* —

JACK.   Calm down, Whitey, I'm fucking with you. Can't you be fucked with a little?

WHITEY.   Not at this hour, Jack. Now, what is the matter?

JACK.   I'm failing, Whitey. I'm not doing the work. I'm behind. I'm behind in everything. I'm fucked, wasted, messed up, scared. It's a mess out there. There's all this *snow*, right, and there's me, and there's no shelter, Whitey, no security, just me and *snow*, me and snow, and I want to scream, to be heard, to wake up the snow or something, I want to scream, 'cause I'm all alone. It's just me. Me and snow. All alone, alone, totally alone, alone — fuck it, you know, umm, hmm, it's like, this whole fucking thing is like, uhh, it's like, *shit*. *(Beat.)* You know?

WHITEY.   I must say, you use language like a *knife*, Jack.

JACK.   Whitey, *fuck* you. Cut the shit. No jokes. This is not a joking matter thing, it's no joke.

WHITEY.   I'm sorry, I'm just tired and —

JACK.   *You're* a fucking joke, Whitey. *You're* the joke. Whitey's the joke. Lonelier than me. Who could have dreamed *you* up, invented *you*? You're the joke. Fool-faggot-fuck isolated in Bumfuckville, surrounded by snow, *drunken*, boozed-up tank of shit, *stupid* shit —

WHITEY.   Stop it, Jack.

JACK.   Make me. Fucking *make* me.

WHITEY.   You're not well. You're drunk and God knows what and you are not well. You should rest, cleanse your system, and we can discuss any problems you may have with me —

JACK.   I'm gone.

WHITEY.   Where are you going? You're improperly dressed.

JACK.   I'm gonna fuck the snow.

WHITEY.   Take one of my jackets.

JACK.   Fuck your jackets, fuck you.

WHITEY.   All right, listen, Jack. I've had enough.

JACK.   Have you had enough? *Huh?* You dumb ugly shit-for-brains? Enough *drink*?

WHITEY.   You can sleep on the couch if you want. If you're not a complete imbecile, you *will*. You'll catch your *death* of cold if you leave here tonight. We can talk in the morning.

JACK.   I want to sleep on the bed.

WHITEY.   *I* am sleeping in my bed.

JACK.   So am I.

WHITEY.   Jack, I do not think —

JACK.   I want to sleep on the fucking bed. I'm sleeping on the fucking bed. I'm not sleeping on the couch.

WHITEY.   Listen, Jack, do whatever you want. I'm too old and too tired. I'm going to sleep. If you want to sleep on the couch, *fine*. If you want to sleep on the bed, that's fine, too. Just so long as you be *quiet* and allow me to *sleep*. I'm exhausted and I need my rest.

JACK.   Are you gonna tell me a bedtime story?

WHITEY.   I'm going to bed. *(Whitey gets into bed. Jack undresses and gets into bed with Whitey.)*

JACK.   Whitey?

WHITEY.   Don't talk, Jack. Just sleep. We'll talk in the morning.

JACK.   I want to kiss you.

WHITEY.   Don't say things like that, Jack.

JACK.   *(Whispers.)* Whitey, listen. I want to fuck you. I'm a faggot, too, Whitey, I'm a fucking faggot, just like you. I want to be just like you, Whitey, I want to be just like you. *(Beat.)* I want to be just like you ... *(The lights fade on Jack, and Whitey moves back to Ex.)*

EX.   That's *crazy*.

WHITEY.   I know.

EX.   The kid is psycho. He's the *movie*. He's *lunatic*.

WHITEY.   I know.

EX.   Deranged.

WHITEY.   I know.

EX.   A-B-C-Deranged. *(Beat.)* What happened then?

WHITEY.   He kept muttering, but finally he fell asleep, and then, finally, thank God, *I* fell asleep.

EX.   What happened in the morning?

WHITEY.   In the morning ... he was gone. *(Beat.)* Along with one of my *coats*.

Scene 4

Robin is typing fast. Ex enters.

EX.   Honey —

ROBIN.   Where were you?

EX.   I was at Whitey's —

ROBIN.   You weren't at dinner. What about talking at dinner? You weren't *there*.

EX.   I had to go over to Whitey's.

ROBIN.   You're more faithful to Whitey than you are to me.

EX.   That's — come on, don't say things like that. You know I love you.

ROBIN.   I *thought* you did.

EX.   What's that supposed to mean?

ROBIN.   It's supposed to mean Sharon's mouth is *big*. It's supposed to mean you shouldn't send tangible items if you don't want to get *caught*, that's what it's supposed to mean. You gave her *flowers*?

EX.   *What*? That's ridiculous, where'd you hear —

ROBIN.   She's *telling* people you gave her flowers. I mean, *enough* that you're having an affair with the stupidest person on this campus, but you're sending her things that you're not even sending *me*. I'm not even asking for exclusivity here, I'm asking for *equality*. *She* gets flowers, the least you could have done was send *me* some flowers. Not that anything would have been *excused*, but do you know how low it makes me feel? Are you aware —

EX.   Robin —

ROBIN.   You sent the tramp *flowers*, Ex. You went to town and gave money to a *florist* so your little affair could smell *flowers.*

EX. *(Beat.)* I called 1-800-FLOWERS. I did not go into town.

ROBIN. You *called.* How thoughtful. You should have called *me.* Perhaps I could have picked out some roses and delivered them for you personally, if I happened to be in the right mood, in the floral *spirit,* as it were.

EX. What can I say? Okay. What can I say?

ROBIN. Goodbye. You can start with good-bye.

EX. Oh, what's that supposed to mean?

ROBIN. It's supposed to mean that I've had enough of this shit. Yes, I know, I asked for it, I do deserve *some* of it because I tolerated it, I *allowed* it, I *ignored* it, but there are limits. You've pulled off some incredible stunts during this relationship, gotten away with extraordinary garbage, and I want to be the first to congratulate you, you do the *scumbag* thing extremely well. But I will no longer be a segment of your vicious circle. I don't fit. I can't even look at myself in the mirror, because when I do, all I can see are *flowers,* somebody else's *flowers.* You've gotten a lot of mileage on just a few drops of romance *very* early on. I'm a sucker. But the tank is empty. Enough of this. I can't do it. Enough.

EX. *(Beat.)* Sorry. *(Beat.)* Whitey's been charged with sexual harassment.

ROBIN. *Excuse* me. What?

EX. Jack Kahn charged Whitey with sexual harassment. There's gonna be a hearing.

ROBIN. Whitey *McCoy?*

EX. Yeah, Whitey McCoy. That's what I came over here to tell you. I wanted to give you a scoop. I thought you might be able to write an article or something. I wanted to let you know. That's why I came. *(Beat.)* Sorry. *(Ex exits.)*

Scene 5

70s music is playing at a party, and Robin and Debbie are standing against a wall. Everybody has to shout to be heard over the music.

DEBBIE.   Unsuspecting good looking transfer student with prep school boyish haircut in my sights, Robin, you'll have to excuse me but it's every woman for herself from this moment on, and every man for *me*. Wish me luck.

ROBIN.   Luck.

DEBBIE.   Same. *(Debbie exits. Willy enters, drinking a beer and holding another.)*

WILLY.   Hey, Robin.

ROBIN.   Hey, Willy.

WILLY.   You want a beer?

ROBIN.   No thanks. I wouldn't want to take your last beer.

WILLY.   I'm covered.

ROBIN.   I wouldn't want to take your second-to-last beer.

WILLY.   I've got four more. This coat has lots of pockets.

ROBIN.   Handy.

WILLY.   J. Crew.

ROBIN.   What?

WILLY.   The coat. It's from J. Crew.

ROBIN.   Oh.

WILLY.   In case you need to find a coat with lots of pockets.

ROBIN.   Thanks for the tip.

WILLY.   I heard about you and Ex.

ROBIN.   What?

WILLY.   I heard you and Ex broke up.

ROBIN.   Who told you that?

WILLY.   Ex.

ROBIN.   Oh. Well, yeah, we broke up.

WILLY.   That's too bad. I'm sorry.

ROBIN.   Thanks.

WILLY.   *(Beat.)* You wanna take a walk? It's kind of loud in here.

ROBIN. Thanks, but I like the music.

WILLY. Yeah, I know. The 70s. Jimmy Carter. Cocaine. Disco. *Xanadu* — Olivia Newton-John on skates. The original Saturday Night Live. Would have been a hell of a lot more fun to go to college in the 70s.

ROBIN. I know what you mean.

WILLY. Sex without condoms. *(Beat.)* You wanna go back to my room?

ROBIN. What?

WILLY. I've got a lot of mix tapes with 70s music back in my room.

ROBIN. *(Beat.)* Are you trying to pick me up, Willy?

WILLY. It may be a little forward sloppy 'cause of the beer — yeah, I'm trying to pick you up.

ROBIN. You're one of Ex's best friends. You're in his band. We just broke up. What are you *thinking*?

WILLY. *(Beat.)* So, you don't want to go back to my room?

ROBIN. No. No, thank you, Willy.

WILLY. Hey, that's totally just fine. That's okay and everything. I'm a healthy English-speaking male with good skin and a car on an isolated campus with two girls for every boy. I'm dating *gold*. I just thought I'd give you a shot at it.

ROBIN. You're like one of the Beach Boys from *hell*. I can't wait to bump into you ten years from now, in the *real* world, Willy. I can't wait to see you when reverse alchemy has turned your dating gold into *shit*.

WILLY. *(Beat.)* Hostile dyke *bitch*. *(Willy exits.)*

ROBIN. Pathetic macho — oh, fuck *you*. That sucks. I hate *that*. *(Igor enters.)*

IGOR. Hey, Robin.

ROBIN. Igor, please don't try to pick me up. This is not the time.

IGOR. I wouldn't even know how to start, Robin, I swear. First of all, trying to find somebody safe on this campus, I mean, somebody who's relatively disease free, who hasn't slept with one of my friends, who isn't heavily involved with somebody, who isn't painful to look at or talk to, who actually likes guys — this is a next-to-impossible task. If I do find somebody like this, the odds that she will have any interest in me are not terrific. And, you know, I mean, I don't even know if I would *allow* myself to go after a person I respected, since I know the kind of guy I am. I know the thoughts I think. I know I would not want *me* to date my daughter, if I had a daughter. I know that I cease to become interested in nine out of ten women almost immediately after I've slept with them, and I've only slept with *three* women. I know I prematurely ejaculate on occasion. I know I sometimes prefer blow jobs to actual intercourse, yet I can't come up with a halfway logical reason for a woman to want to give one. I know I find sleazy women pretty attractive, and look at most women as objects. I know that white men have a hell of a historical legacy, what with enslaving blacks and treating women like cattle, so I feel ashamed to be a member of what is supposed to be the privileged class. And I know that sensitive guys sound good in theory, but in practice, most of the women I observe are attracted to men who treat them like shit. I know these things. So, you see, it would be very difficult for me to try to pick you up while retaining even *minor* amounts of dignity and truth and still enjoy myself a little. *(Beat.)* But I was standing over there, across the room, and I saw Willy try to pick you up, and I know he's pretty smashed tonight, and I just wanted to see if you were okay. *(Beat.)* Are you okay?

ROBIN. I'm okay. *(Beat.)* Have you been drinking tonight, Igor?

IGOR. A little.

ROBIN. You guys should seriously consider wearing those Mickey Mouse Club T-shirts with your names on them, because it's getting difficult to tell you all *apart.*

IGOR. Understandably. I mean, we're all heterosexual white guys in college who play music and don't understand women. But there are subtle differences. Ex has the most money, Willy is the most obnoxious, and I'm the most introspective.

ROBIN. Still, I think Mickey Mouse T-shirts would be a good idea. Just a thought.

Scene 6

Quintana is at her desk. Igor enters.

IGOR.   Xavier Reynolds, President Matheson.

QUINTANA.   Yes. *(Igor exits. Ex enters and shuts the door.)*

EX.   Hello, President Matheson.

QUINTANA.   Call me Quintana, please.

EX.   I'd prefer President Matheson, if you don't mind.

QUINTANA.   I don't mind.

EX.   May I sit down?

QUINTANA.   Certainly. *(Ex sits.)* Now, what can I do for you today?

EX.   You can tell me what the hell is going on around here.

QUINTANA.   I'm afraid you're going to have to be a bit more specific than that, Xavier.

EX.   Call me Mister Reynolds, please.

QUINTANA.   Certainly, Mister Reynolds. What, specifically, can I tell you?

EX.   You can tell me why this school is persecuting Whitey McCoy.

QUINTANA.   I can assure you the college is not *persecuting* anybody, but I'm afraid I can't really say much more about that matter at this time, as I am currently involved in the on-going process —

EX.   You're killing this place. Ever since you took over, you've had this conservative *plan*. Whitey's an aberration. He doesn't fit in with your *plan*. He's homosexual. He's alcoholic. Too bad he's not Jewish and black and crippled as well. You'd really have a *field* day, then. "So *what* if he's a tenured professor who's given almost twenty years of his life to this place? So *what*? He's a 'bad apple'." A healthy society *deals* with problems. It doesn't toss them away and shut the door. God forbid Whitey *did* what this kid *says* he did. If so, he's got *serious* problems and needs *help*. And *treatment*. He's given a big

19

chunk of his life to this school, and he should not be *bullied*, and then ejected as if he were sitting in James Bond's *car*.

QUINTANA. *(Beat.)* Are you done?

EX. For the moment, yes.

QUINTANA. Because if you'd like to continue, please do so. I'm always willing to hear a student speak his or her mind. That's my job.

EX. I'm glad you clarified that, because I thought your job was ruining people's *lives.*

QUINTANA. I'm sorry you feel that way. *(Beat.)* If that's all you have to say to me right now, I think we should wrap this up. My schedule is full to bursting these days, as I'm sure you can imagine, Mister Reynolds.

EX. Xavier, please.

QUINTANA. *Xavier.*

EX. See you, Prez. *(Ex starts to go.)* Hey, Prez.

QUINTANA. Yes.

EX. You know what I just realized?

QUINTANA. What's that?

EX. Your blinds are drawn. That's interesting.

QUINTANA. I'm glad you find that interesting, Xavier.

EX. Because, you know, the blinds have been drawn, the door has been shut, and only you and I have been inside your office. I could walk out of here, you know, I could undo my pants and *run* out of here, and I could accuse *you* of trying to molest me. After all, who's to say you didn't? Am I right? It would be your word against mine. Word Versus Word. Meryl Streep and Dustin Hoffman can *portray* us in *Word Versus Word.* Could make a good flick. A student against a figure-in-power. Sound familiar?

QUINTANA. Extremely. *(Beat.)* Do whatever you feel you *need* to do, Xavier. I hope you prepare for the outcome of whatever actions you choose, however, because I'm very, very good at my job, and I'd advise you not to play games you're not up for.

EX. I'm full tuition, Prez.

QUINTANA. All students receive equal consideration, and I

resent the implication. Now, if you'll excuse me, I'm very busy, Xavier.

EX.   We're *all* of us busy in one way. Or another. *Later.* *(Ex exits.)*

Scene 7

Jack is standing alone.

JACK.   This is how it happened. Thanksgiving break, most everybody away from the campus, at home, visiting friends, anything to escape the empty cold of this place during a vacation. Some stayed behind to do work and some stayed behind ... just because. I wasn't getting on well with my folks then, I didn't want to go back home. I was tinkering around with a sculpture project. It wasn't like I was just twiddling my thumbs. I took Whitey's philosophy course that term. I wanted an extension on a paper. The paper wasn't late yet, I just thought I could do a better job on it if I had a little extra time, another week or so. One night, walking alone down the road, I saw the light in his apartment on. I headed over there. He always told a bunch of us guys to stop by whenever we felt like it, told us he'd give us stuff to eat and drink, whatever. Yeah, it was weird, him being our teacher, but a few times we took him up on it, and it was fine. He'd play music for us and give us beers and grill us sandwiches, fancy, not something simple like peanut butter. We'd always leave early. It could get really depressing. Whitey would get this sad look in his eyes, lonely, and he'd be soused, way drunk, which didn't help. But Thanksgiving night, his light was on, and I figured it was a good idea to ask for the extension. I mean, it was Thanksgiving, you know? I rang his bell, and he came to the door, wearing pajama bottoms and an enormous T-shirt. He'd been drinking, I could smell that, so I said maybe I should come back some other time. *(Whitey enters.)*

WHITEY.   No, no, it's fine, come on in, come in, come in.

JACK.   He closed the door after me and locked it.

WHITEY.   Cold out there. It's eerie up here this time of year, nobody around. Don't you think?

JACK.   Sure. *(To audience.)* He tried to get me drunk, bring me down to his level.

WHITEY.   Something to drink?

JACK.   No, thanks.

WHITEY.   Oh, don't be so *stiff.*

JACK.   Maybe just a beer, thanks.

WHITEY.   Drink some vodka with me. It'll warm your insides.

JACK.   Umm ...

WHITEY.   Top-of-the-line. Stoli.

JACK.   Okay. *(Whitey pours two shots. Jack and Whitey each drink one. Whitey pours two more shots. Jack and Whitey each drink one. Whitey pours two more shots. Jack and Whitey each drink one.)* Whitey, I wanted to talk to you about my paper —

WHITEY.   Take off your clothes.

JACK.   Excuse me?

WHITEY.   Take off your clothes.

JACK.   Whitey, I think —

WHITEY.   Take off your clothes. Off with those fucking clothes. I want you naked. I want you to be fucking naked.

JACK.   *(To audience.)* He was cursing at me ... and he was very intimidating. I was terrified. The door was locked. I —

WHITEY.   Take off your clothes.

JACK.   I think I should go.

WHITEY.   If you try to leave, you're going to die.

JACK.   I ...

WHITEY.   Take off your clothes. Now.

JACK.   *(To audience.)* I obliged. I took off everything but my underpants. *(Jack undresses.)*

WHITEY.   Much better. You look much *better.* Oh, *yes.* Look at your little body. Look at your little skin. Young skin. Little body. Young Bird. My Thanksgiving turkey.

JACK.   *(To audience.)* I couldn't believe what I was hearing. I wanted to scream, but I was petrified he'd kill me. His kitchen was fully stocked with sharp knives, hanging and gleaming, the same knives he used when he'd cut our grilled sandwiches. I thought he would cut me. I should have screamed. But who would have heard me? I just kept thinking: How can I live? How can I survive this? Will I have to figure out a way to kill him? Am I going to die?

WHITEY.   Get on the bed.

JACK.   Whitey, please —

WHITEY.   I want you in the bed. Inside the bed.

JACK.   I can't do this —

WHITEY.   Act like a *man*, for Christ-fucking-sakes. Be a *man*.

JACK.   I can't —

WHITEY.   On the bed. *(Jack gets on the bed.)* I'm going to swallow you. I'm going to put you in my mouth. And then you're going to put me in your mouth. We're going to help one another. Understand? Help one another. *(The lights fade on Whitey, and Jack is alone again.)*

JACK.   I ... I don't know if I can continue talking about ... I ... this is ... you have to understand, this is very hard for me. Very difficult. This was ... this *is* ... this is the worst thing that's ever happened to me. It's still ... very tough to put it into words. It still makes me ashamed. *(Beat.)* He ... he blew me. He performed oral sex *upon* me. He wanted me to reciprocate. I wouldn't. I couldn't. I brought him to orgasm ... manually. With my ... with my *hand*. With *this* hand. It was a compromise. I don't know how I was even able to do that. I was sickened. Once he ... finished, he fell asleep ... passed out ... in a drunken stupor. I was able to escape. And I didn't know what to do. I hated myself. I hated him. I avoided him. Never handed in my philosophy paper. He passed me anyway. He would keep trying to talk to me, keep trying to get me alone with him, but I never let it happen again. I kept my distance. And I kept my mouth shut. Until — until I couldn't keep it inside me any longer. Until now. *(Beat.)* This is how it happened. *(Quintana enters.)*

QUINTANA.   Thank you, Jack.

Emotional

Scene 8

Whitey is drinking vodka, Robin is interviewing him with a tape recorder.

ROBIN.   What will you do?

WHITEY.   What *can* I do? Leave. Pack up eighteen years of my life and sweep the floor for the next fool. I phoned a moving company today to find out how much it would cost to move my belongings into storage. You wouldn't believe the amount I was quoted. *Gods* should do the moving for the money they ask for. I have to pack up all the beautiful books on my shelves. My *library*. I can't afford to move my books. I don't know where the money will come from. I could never save money on my salary. If only I had been born into a wealthy family, I could have actually afforded to *teach* here. Only the wealthy can afford to teach, and only the wealthy can afford to study. It's all about money. *(Whitey drinks his vodka, then refills the glass.)*

ROBIN.   You're drinking a lot.

WHITEY.   This has not yet turned on me. This has not yet betrayed me. I still have this. *(Beat.)* Eighteen years of teaching, not once has anybody so much as thought to accuse me of such a thing. Along comes this self-hating baby who can't come to terms with his own sexuality, whose name can't be printed in your paper because he's the supposed *victim.* He is no victim. *I* am the victim here. Two people know the truth. I know the truth and that crazy liar knows the truth, and our words *conflict.* Based on *that,* a decision was made by their *committee,* but they stalled it, waited until graduation was done, when all the students had left for the summer, *two days* after graduation, they told me. They knew all along. But they didn't want to create a stir. No fuss, no mess, because, you see, *I'm* mess. Nobody sticks their neck out on my behalf, because they're terrified their jobs will be the next to go, these supposedly fearless academic minds, cowering in corners, afraid of being *spanked*. *(Beat.)* This is my life, *I* know the truth. How can a judgment be made?

ROBIN.   They say the judgment was based on the testimony and on character —

WHITEY.   *Character?* One person is a drug-addicted, confused young girl of a man, the other is a tenured professor. *He* has character? He deserves what he claims to have gotten, he deserves worse, this bastion of "character." *(Whitey drinks his vodka, then refills the glass.)*

ROBIN.   Whitey, would you please look into my eyes for a moment? *(Whitey looks into Robin's eyes.)* Did you do this?

WHITEY.   *(Beat.) No.* I did not. No.

ROBIN.   *(Beat.)* I still don't know. I can't tell. For the life of me, I can't tell. You were right. Two people know the truth, and your stories conflict. *Two* truths? Or none at all? I can't tell. I cannot tell. *(Beat.)* Umm, this interview won't be published until September. It'll be in the first issue of next school year's paper. I'm sorry about the delay, but —

WHITEY.   Don't apologize. I appreciate your effort. You stayed around and you didn't have to. Don't apologize. *(Beat.)* Better late than never. Right? Better late … you know, that, that … that *young man* would always walk into my class a little bit late. Five minutes, fifteen minutes. There are always a few students who can't seem to get there right on time. I'd always think to myself, as they straggled in, "Better late than never." But with that young man, in hindsight, I think it would have been better the other way around. *(Whitey drinks his vodka. Robin shuts off her tape recorder.)*

ROBIN.   Goodbye, Whitey.

WHITEY.   Enjoy your summer. *(Beat.)* I've been saying that to students for eighteen years. Enjoy your summer.

ROBIN.   You, too. Enjoy yours.

WHITEY.   Thank you.

ROBIN.   Good luck.

WHITEY.   Thank you.

ROBIN.   *(Beat.)* I can't *tell*. *(Robin exits quickly.)*

Scene 9

Ex and Igor are hanging Christmas lights on the wall. Willy walks in.

WILLY.   I hear Whitey got another job.

IGOR.   Where?

WILLY.   Playing Santa Claus at a shopping mall.

IGOR.   Wow.

EX.   No way.

WILLY.   It's what I heard.

EX.   It's probably a rumor. Jack Kahn probably spread it.

WILLY.   It's what I heard.

IGOR.   *(To Ex.)* Have you talked to Whitey lately?

EX.   Nah, not for a while.

IGOR.   It's weird …

WILLY.   *What's* weird?

IGOR.   Whitey was a presence here for so long. And then all this stuff happens. And then he's gone. And it's like, yeah, it's a big deal for a few days, but then everybody gets involved in their classes or their social lives or themselves, and it's like the whole thing never *happened*. It's like a *footnote*.

WILLY.   *What's* like a footnote?

IGOR.   Weren't you listening —

WILLY.   I'm fucking with you. I know what you're talking about. But the problem of the thing is, like, nobody fucking knows, and none of us has half a clue about legality and what it's all about from that standpoint, so the thing *dies. (Beat.)* I mean, he could have definitely screwed the kid, you know? It's not *so* unlikely.

EX.   He didn't.

WILLY.   Yeah, but you don't *know* that.

EX.   He *told* me he didn't. His *word.*

WILLY.   And Jack Kahn told somebody else something different … gave *his* word … and therein lies the fucking heartbeat of the problem. The guy was lonely, drunk, nobody to love —

EX.   *Which* guy?

WILLY. *Either* guy. It doesn't matter. Hell, if I were Whitey, alone with a guy on a cold night, I probably would've screwed him, too.

EX.   He was never even accused of screwing him, he was accused of sucking him off.

WILLY.   The kid got a blow job and he's complaining. Some nerve.

EX.   An *alleged* blow job.

WILLY.   An alleged blow job's better than no blow job.

IGOR.   *(Beat.)* A drop of reality tossed into the middle of things sure provided some perspective around this place for a while there.

WILLY.   Yeah. I'm glad things are back to normal.

IGOR.   *(Beat.)* Does anybody feel like rehearsing?

WILLY.   We're seniors, we don't have to *rehearse.*

IGOR.   *Seriously,* do you guys feel like rehearsing or don't you?

EX.   *Eventually ...*

Scene 10

A slow, sad, instrumental Christmas song plays in the dark. The lights abruptly come up as the music shifts to unthreatening, tinkly shopping mall music. Whitey is seen in a dim spotlight, dressed as Santa Claus without the white beard and holding a small liquor bottle.

WHITEY.   *(Sings.)* "Chestnuts roasting on an open fire, Jack Frost nipping at your nose ... nipping at your nose ... nipping at your nose ... nipping at your nose ..." *(The melody fades away, and Whitey sounds like a broken record. He continues to sing, the words sounding almost mechanical, as the lights fade to black.)*

END OF ACT ONE

ACT TWO

Scene 1

In the darkness, we hear the end of a commercial and the beginning of a television news theme song. The lights slowly rise. There is a small portable TV on the floor, center stage. To the left are Robin and Debbie, sitting on Robin's bed, drinking wine. To the right are Ex and Willy, drinking beer. Willy is sitting on the floor, leaning against Ex's bed. Ex is sprawled across his bed, playing with the sort of plastic toy gun that shoots rubber suction cup darts. During the following, he puts the gun to his temple, inside his mouth, to the back of Willy's head, towards the TV, and so on. The students' dialogue and the TV dialogue can overlap throughout.

HELENA. *(TV.)* I'm Helena Marx, and you're watching the 6 o'clock news on WRGB. In local news tonight, a former professor has filed a lawsuit against the college where he taught for eighteen years until he was fired last June, when a student claimed he had been sexually harassed by the professor, who is here with us tonight. This is former professor Whitey McCoy. Mr. McCoy, thank you for being with us tonight.
WHITEY. *(TV.)* Thank you, Helena. *(Robin is searching for her tape recorder.)*
WILLY. Holy shit.
DEBBIE. *This* whole thing again?
HELENA. *(TV.)* Why exactly are you suing the college?
WHITEY. *(TV.)* They ruined my life. With very little cause. They held a slapdash hearing, promptly dismissed me, and gave me a week to vacate the apartment that's been my home for eighteen years. The only person I could appeal to was the same person that made the decision to fire me, the college

28

president. There wasn't even a transcript of my hearing. I thought I must have some basic rights of due process in the situation.

WILLY.   He's *drunk*. Probably knocked back a few of these *(Shakes his beer can.)* right before the cameras rolled.

EX.   *Vodka* was his drink. He mostly drank *vodka*. *(Robin holds her tape recorder up to the TV speaker.)*

DEBBIE.   What are you doing?

ROBIN.   I want to get this on tape.

WILLY.   Nice tie.

EX.   That *is* a nice tie.

HELENA.   *(TV.)* Are you looking to be reinstated, or do you seek monetary damages?

WHITEY.   *(TV.)* Helena, I love that college. But, unfortunately, it's no longer an amenable environment for me. I am suing the college for damages, most of which will go to my lawyers, who have agreed to take the case on a contingency basis. Above all else, I want to clear my name. It's really all I've got.

HELENA.   *(TV.)* Thank you for being with us, Mr. McCoy.

WHITEY.   *(TV.)* Thank *you*, Helena. *(Igor runs into Ex's room.)*

IGOR.   Whitey's suing the school!

WILLY.   Thanks for the news flash, Igor. Why don't you watch some TV? *(Igor looks at the TV and catches a glimpse of Whitey.)*

IGOR.   Oh. *(Beat.)* Think he'll win?

EX.   I *hope* so. He still owes me five bucks.

IGOR.   You guys want to go to the snack bar?

WILLY.   Too cold.

EX.   I am hungry, though.

WILLY.   So am I. But it's too *cold.*

IGOR.   I'll bring you guys back something if you want.

EX.   You're a prince among men, Igor, you really are.

WILLY.   I think I'm too drunk to walk.

IGOR.   I don't mind. Katie's working behind the counter tonight.

EX.   Who's Katie? That hot girl with the crazy hair?

WILLY.   And the big tits?

IGOR.   Yeah. *(In a flash, Ex and Willy are up and putting on their coats.)*

EX. Shut the TV off, Willy.

ROBIN. Would you shut that off for me, Debbie?

DEBBIE. Sure. *(Willy and Debbie go towards the TV. Ex shoots a dart at Willy's back. Debbie shuts off the TV.)*

WILLY. Cut it out.

EX. You didn't even see it coming.

WILLY. Yeah, that's very impressive, the old In-The-Back-When-The-Guy's-Not-Looking trick. *(Willy turns around and goes to shut off the TV, but it's already off. He looks confused.)* Huh. *(Beat.)* That's weird. *(Beat.)* I am *drunk.*

EX. Last one to the snack bar is a rotten egg. *(Willy runs out the door, followed closely by Ex. Debbie and Robin, who have put on their coats, walk out after the boys. The last one to leave is Igor, who closes the door behind him.)*

Scene 2

Quintana is at her desk, a red ribbon prominently displayed on her clothing. Igor enters.

IGOR. Robin Smith, President Matheson.

QUINTANA. Yes. *(Igor exits. Robin enters with her tape recorder.)*

ROBIN. Hello, President Matheson.

QUINTANA. *Quintana,* please.

ROBIN. Thank you, Quintana, for seeing me on such short notice. I know how busy you must —

QUINTANA. It's always a pleasure to talk to a *student.* Especially such a *distinguished* student. I hear you're going to deliver the valedictory speech at commencement.

ROBIN. Yes, I —

QUINTANA. Congratulations.

ROBIN. Thank you —

QUINTANA. You must be very proud.

ROBIN.   Yes, I am, thanks, but — with all due respect —
that's not what I came here to talk with you about, and since
I know how busy you must be —
QUINTANA.   "With all due respect." A loaded phrase. Since
the amount of respect actually *due* is never specified, and so
left up to the discretion of ... *whomever.*
ROBIN.   *(Beat.) Touché. (Beat.)* Now — you don't mind if I
record our conversation, do you?
QUINTANA.   Not at all.
ROBIN.   Great. *(Robin turns her tape recorder on.)* Okay. *Now.*
(Beat.) Do you believe that the college deprived Whitey McCoy
of the basic rights of due process?
QUINTANA.   Well, due process applies to *public* trials, and
the college is a *private* institution, but beyond that, I'm not
really able to comment, since I am currently involved in the
legal proceedings brought against the school by Mr. McCoy
and his lawyers.
ROBIN.   Why was there no transcript of the hearing the
college held involving the case?
QUINTANA.   I'm afraid I'm not able to comment on that
either, since it is part of the lawsuit.
ROBIN.   Do you think Whitey McCoy was a competent
professor? I mean, *before* this whole issue came about?
QUINTANA.   I can't really answer that right now.
ROBIN.   Are you *sure* you want to do this interview?
QUINTANA.   *(Beat.) Absolutely. (Beat.)* After all, the school
newspaper exists for the benefit of the *students,* and so do I.
And I am more than happy to answer any questions I can.
(Beat. Robin looks out the window.)
ROBIN.   How do you feel about the seasonal change from
winter into spring?
QUINTANA.   Excuse me?
ROBIN.   Well, you can't really talk about any of the things
I came here to talk to you about, and I'm not really prepared
to talk about anything *else,* so I suppose we might as well talk
about the *weather.*
QUINTANA.   I *see. (Pause.)* I *know* I must seem like this re-
actionary authority figure, nothing more nor less. I know that's

how I'm perceived. *(Beat.)* I sometimes wish each student could step into my shoes and run this institution for even fifteen *minutes*, see what it means ... to try running something valid — something *valuable* — in today's world, in this climate. It is not as ideal or simple as you — or I — would have it be. *(Beat.)* You brought up the weather. Okay, let's talk about the weather. Let's imagine what it would be like if constantly, throughout the year — not just four times, not just Winter-Spring-Summer-Fall but *all the time*, everything around you changed and kept on changing. It's your responsibility to deal authoritatively with each change, while not taking so much time that you're unable to deal with the *next* change when it arises.... You try to be as fair as possible, but — inevitably — somebody feels slighted, not everybody is satisfied, not everybody accepts your judgments. Your *judgments*. Because you *have* to make judgments, you simply *have* to. Or nothing gets done. *(Beat.)* You do the best you can, based on what you believe to be true, based on what your experience, your knowledge, your *life* tells you is true, and you hope beyond hope that the failures you *do* have — and you *will* have failures — well, you hope beyond hope that your failures will *enlighten* you, rather than *destroy* you. *(Beat. Quintana looks out the window.)* My husband wouldn't mind spending the rest of his life in one place — in one *chair*, or so sometimes it seems — but as for me, I cannot travel enough. I love going to new places, *exploring*.... And yet, I'll tell you: There is nothing like springtime in New England.

Scene 3

Ex reads the school newspaper, Willy fills a squirt gun with Cran-Blueberry juice from a bottle, Igor eats sesame noodles from a white Chinese take-out container.

EX. Looks like we got some competition, boys.

WILLY. What do you mean?

EX. Listen up: "Rough and tumble grunge music on CD for the ridiculously low price of eight bucks. Pick up a copy of *Postmodern Nasal Drip Dry* by Venison. Or don't. See if we care."

WILLY. Eight bucks for something called *Postmodern Nasal Drip Dry*? Are you shitting me?

EX. Read it and weep. *(Ex hands Willy the paper.)*

WILLY. What the fuck is Venison?

EX. The flesh of a deer.

WILLY. Answer my question.

EX. Five freshman guys. They think they're a band.

WILLY. With a name like *Venison*? Venison's the flesh of a deer, not a band.

EX. You're telling *me*.

WILLY. *Which* five freshman guys?

EX. You know, they played right after Thanksgiving last year.

WILLY. With the tall lead singer?

EX. Six-five or something.

WILLY. *Those guys* put out a CD? Those guys *suck*.

EX. Well, for eight bucks, you can hear them suck *digitally*.

WILLY. Name me *one* good band with a singer that tall. *One* band.

EX. The Los Angeles Lakers.

WILLY. A *band*.

EX. The Boston Celtics.

WILLY. A *band*.

EX. Your mother.

WILLY. Shut up. *(Beat.)* Six foot, five inches tall. *(Beat.)* Probably hung like a horse race.

EX.   You know the saying: It's not the size of the meat, it's the motion of the ocean.

WILLY.   You got a small dick too, huh?

EX.   Ask your mother.

WILLY.   Shut up. *(Beat.)* Hey, Igor, give me some of that.

IGOR.   Huh?

WILLY.   Share the wealth, my friend.

IGOR.   What?

WILLY.   Can — I — have — some — of — your — Chinese — food — please?

IGOR.   Oh, yeah. Here. *(Willy takes the food and eats it with his hands.)*

WILLY.   This is ice cold.

IGOR.   It's supposed to be. Sesame noodles.

WILLY.   It's like spaghetti or something. It should be hot.

IGOR.   Think of it as the noodle equivalent of gazpacho.

WILLY.   I *hate* gazpacho.

EX.   I hate your mother.

WILLY.   Shut up.

EX.   *(To Igor.)* Hey, Silent Man, you're being awful quiet. What's on your mind?

IGOR.   Oh, no, nothing, I was just … you know, I was just thinking about everything I don't know how to do.

WILLY.   Is that possible? Can you think about something without being able to do it?

EX.   Yeah, Einstein, I can think about fucking your mother … oh, that's not a good example, I can *do* that.

WILLY.   Shut up.

EX.   *(To Igor.)* What can't you do?

IGOR.   Most everything. I can't *sew*, I can't *cook*, I can't *surf*, I can't *swim* … or play a stringed instrument, fix a car, make a fire with two sticks. Fold colored paper into little origami animal shapes. Build a house. Make a noose. Survive in the woods. Do my own taxes. *(Beat.)* Be friends with a girl. *(Beat.)* Lots of stuff. *(Beat.)* I mean, what if I were the last man on Earth? All of civilization's accomplishments would be lost.

EX.   You can do all sorts of things.

IGOR.   Like what?

EX.   Like play the drums.

IGOR.   I suck. I'm worse than Ringo Starr.

WILLY.   You *do* suck.

EX.   Ringo Starr's underrated.

WILLY.   You're pretty good at hanging out with us.

IGOR.   What good is that going to do me if I'm the last man on Earth? I can hang out with the guys, great, only there won't be any guys to hang out with.

WILLY.   What is this last man on Earth hypothetical pantywaist bullshit, Igor? The odds of you being the last man on Earth are not so hot.

IGOR.   I just hate taking other people for granted, relying on other people in order to live my life.

WILLY.   Oh, get off it. Join the tribe.

IGOR.   I'm serious, Willy.

EX.   I'm serious too, Willy. About your mother.

WILLY.   Shut up.

EX.   You're an integral part of this band, Igor.

IGOR.   We don't even have a *name*.

EX.   *(Pause.)* We don't *need* one.

WILLY.   That's right.

EX.   Names are for pussies.

WILLY.   Venison needs a name, we don't.

EX.   Our music speaks for itself.

IGOR.   *What* music? We barely ever *play* music.

EX.   We pace ourselves. You know that.

WILLY.   Fucking *A*, we pace ourselves.

EX.   There's always the danger of over-rehearsing, losing our spontaneity, our edge, our *je ne sais quoi*.

IGOR.   *What je ne sais quoi?* We sit here belittling other bands while Willy squirts cranberry juice into his mouth.

WILLY.   Cran-*Blueberry* juice, Mr. Juice Expert Man, Cran-*Blueberry*.

IGOR.   It's just — we're all graduating soon and — I ... I ...

WILLY.   You *what?*

EX.   You *what?*

IGOR.   I guess I quit. *(Igor exits.)*

EX.   *(Beat.)* Pass me those sesame noodles.

WILLY.   He'll be back.

EX.   He's probably just tense about graduating.

WILLY.   What's he gonna do — put out a solo CD? Igor Konigsberg plays the *beats* to your favorite songs. That'd probably be *real* popular on campus. He could probably charge eight-fifty for that. Knock Venison right off the charts.

EX.   Maybe *we* should put out a CD.

WILLY.   *(Beat.)* Yeah, maybe. *(Beat.)* We'd probably have to name the band first. Not that I think we *need* a name, but so they'd know where to put us in the record stores.

EX.   We could always just call ourselves *Your Mother.*

WILLY.   Shut up, Ex. I mean it. Shut up.

Scene 4

Slow jazz plays. Debbie stares at a goldfish in a bowl, Robin writes on a pad of paper. They each have a glass of wine.

DEBBIE.   Come on.

ROBIN.   No, thank you. I have to work on this. Besides, everybody's getting too weird out there. It happens every year, a week before it's all over, all of a sudden people are sleeping with somebody they've always hated, or getting into fights with their best friends. I'll leave it all to you.

DEBBIE.   Tina's boyfriend brought some cute friends of his from Williams. They'll probably be at the party.

ROBIN.   Send my regards.

DEBBIE.   Why are you working so hard on that thing? All you've gotta do is stand up, say Good Riddance, Nice Knowing You, Tra-La-La, and walk away.

ROBIN.   You should be making this speech, Debbie, you've got such a way with words. *(There is a knock on the door.)* Who is it?

IGOR.   *(Off.)* Igor!

ROBIN.   Igor?

IGOR.   *(Off.)* Igor!

ROBIN.   Come in! *(Igor enters.)*

IGOR.   Hi, Robin. Hi, Debbie.

DEBBIE.   Hi, Igor.

IGOR.   Hi.

DEBBIE.   Hi.

IGOR.   Hi.

ROBIN.   What's going on, Igor?

IGOR.   I was, uh, I was wondering if I could talk to you for a minute, but if you're busy —

DEBBIE.   No, no, three's a crowd, I was just leaving, some of us have a party to go to.

IGOR.   I was just there.

DEBBIE.   How is it?

IGOR.   Pretty good. Tina's boyfriend brought some cute friends of his from Williams. They're there.

DEBBIE.   What?

IGOR.   I couldn't help overhearing. I've been standing by the door for about a minute.

ROBIN.   What were you doing eavesdropping, Igor?

IGOR.   It was not intentional, I was trying to, you know, stand up. Balance. Stay sort of vertical. I've had a few drinks.

DEBBIE.   Is there still beer over there?

IGOR.   I think so. I wasn't drinking beer.

DEBBIE.   What were you drinking?

IGOR.   Wine and vodka. Glass of wine, shot of vodka, glass of wine, shot of vodka, wine, vodka, wine, vodka. You know, always mix, always worry. I'm a worry-wart. A drunken worry-wart. Can I sit down, Robin?

ROBIN.   Sure. *(Igor sits.)*

DEBBIE.   I'm off. Thanks for the wine, Robin.

ROBIN.   You don't have to leave, Debbie —

DEBBIE.   No, no, that's okay. I'll find some freshman boy to kiss, don't worry about me. Ciao.

ROBIN.   Bye.

IGOR.   *Ciao.*

DEBBIE.   *(To the fish.)* Take care of yourself, Anastasia. *(Debbie exits.)*

IGOR. *(Beat.)* Your fish is named Anastasia?

ROBIN. Yeah.

IGOR. The name is bigger than the fish.

ROBIN. She'll grow into it.

IGOR. I suppose so. Or else she'll die and you'll have to flush her down the toilet. *(Beat.)* I'm sorry. That wasn't very thoughtful. I shouldn't imagine fatal scenarios for your pet.

ROBIN. Why do you worry so much, Igor?

IGOR. If I didn't worry, what would I do? *(Beat.)* I'm kind of used to worrying. It's comforting, in a way. People know me for it. Igor Worries. It's my niche. Do you mind if I have some wine?

ROBIN. Not at all. *(Igor pours himself a glass of wine and drinks it, then pours another.)* Why do you drink so much, Igor?

IGOR. Oh. *(Beat.)* Uhh ... *(Beat.)* You know, I like waking up late in a spinning room with a foul tasting dry mouth and a churning empty stomach. Drinking's just a means to an end. *(Igor drinks the rest of the wine in his glass.)*

ROBIN. *(Beat.)* What did you want to talk to me about, Igor?

IGOR. The band broke up, you know.

ROBIN. No, I didn't know that, actually. When?

IGOR. A while ago. I guess there's not all that much difference between the band together and the band broken up.

ROBIN. What happened?

IGOR. You ask a lot of questions.

ROBIN. Does that bother you?

IGOR. That's another question!

ROBIN. I'm a reporter.

IGOR. Oh, yeah, I almost forgot. That's why I came here. *That's* what I wanted to talk to you about. They're going to settle Whitey's case.

ROBIN. *What?*

IGOR. The school. They're going to pay Whitey off, so the case won't go to court. I work in the president's office. The school's lawyers are advising them to settle. Do you mind if I lie down?

ROBIN. Ummm ... *(Igor lies down.)*

IGOR. I just ... don't want to be who I am ... you ever know that feeling ... feel that way ... I just ... don't want to ...

ROBIN. Do you know anything else about the settlement, Igor?

IGOR. Questions ... smells so nice.... Why do women's beds ... so nice ... Anastasia ... The Fish. *(Igor is now fast asleep on the bed. Robin covers him with her blanket, then sits looking at him as the music plays.)*

Scene 5

Ex and Debbie are kissing on his bed. His hands are hidden underneath her shirt.

EX. You have hair there.

DEBBIE. Why? Do you hate that?

EX. Oh, no, I love unshaved underarms. My Mom's from France. *(They kiss.)*

DEBBIE. Ex — Ex — Ex —

EX. Debbie, Debbie, Debbie —

DEBBIE. I feel weird about this.

EX. You do?

DEBBIE. Yeah, a little.

EX. Why?

DEBBIE. Robin's a friend of mine.

EX. Mine, too. What's the matter?

DEBBIE. Well, the two of you —

EX. Went out for a while and then she broke up with me and we no longer go out. What's wrong?

DEBBIE. I just — don't know if this would make her too happy.

EX. She's not here. Why should this be about her? You're here. I'm here. Robin's not here. Are you having fun?

DEBBIE. Yes, *and* feeling *insanely* guilty.

EX. What can I do to make you feel less insanely guilty?

Promise that I won't say anything?

DEBBIE. It's not that, Ex —

EX. Listen, Debbie. I've always liked you —

DEBBIE. I've always liked you, too. I really have always liked you. But I still don't know if this is such a good thing to be doing. This place can be such an incestuous little fishbowl ...

EX. Debbie?

DEBBIE. Yeah?

EX. Can I continue kissing you?

DEBBIE. *Ex* ...

EX. Okay, okay. *(Beat.)* You want something to drink?

DEBBIE. Sure.

EX. What do you want?

DEBBIE. What do you have?

EX. Jack Daniels, tequila, wine, beer —

DEBBIE. What are you gonna drink?

EX. J.D.

DEBBIE. That's fine. *(Ex gets out a bottle of Jack Daniels. He takes a slug and passes it to Debbie, who also takes a slug.)*

EX. So. *(Pause.)* What do you feel like talking about?

DEBBIE. I'm sorry I'm being like this, it's just —

EX. No, hey. I *completely* understand. *(Beat.)* Since we can't act upon our impulses, why don't we talk about them? You know, get rid of some of the tension. What would you like to do if we could do anything, you and I?

DEBBIE. You mean like fantasy stuff or just regular things?

EX. Anything. Fantasy stuff, sure. Fantasies. Tell me your fantasy. If we could do anything.

DEBBIE. I can't.

EX. Sure you can.

DEBBIE. No, I can't.

EX. Why not?

DEBBIE. Because then you'd do it.

EX. What?

DEBBIE. You'd do it.

EX. Debbie, I give you my word as a gentleman and a scholar. Whatever you say, it's just something *said*, it's not something I'd have to *act* upon.

40

DEBBIE. But you would. If I told you, you would.

EX. I swear, there is nothing you could tell me that I would *have* to act upon.

DEBBIE. I don't believe you.

EX. Try me.

DEBBIE. *(Beat.)* You promise not to do it?

EX. Scout's honor.

DEBBIE. Were you a scout?

EX. I'm pretty sure I was, yes.

DEBBIE. *(Beat.)* What's *your* fantasy?

EX. I asked you first.

DEBBIE. That's juvenile.

EX. That's fair and you know it. Tell me.

DEBBIE. My fantasy?

EX. Yeah.

DEBBIE. And you won't act on it?

EX. Nope.

DEBBIE. Okay. *(Beat.)* Okay. *(Beat.)* My fantasy — is to be taken against my will. *(Beat.)* By you. *(Beat. Ex aggressively kisses Debbie.)* Ex, stop it — *(He gets on top of her.)* Ex ... Ex.... Stop — *(He starts to take off her clothing.)* Stop it, Ex. I mean it.

EX. No, you don't ...

DEBBIE. Yes, I do. *Stop it.*

EX. It's your fantasy.

DEBBIE. *Stop it right now, I mean it. (Ex stops and looks at Debbie. He grabs the bottle of Jack Daniels, takes a slug, and hands it to Debbie. She takes a slug and adjusts her clothes. There is a knock on the door.)*

EX. Yeah! *(Willy enters, carrying a bong and a bottle of Jack Daniels.)*

WILLY. If the man cannot be found at the party, the party will find the man!

DEBBIE. I should go.

WILLY. There's plenty here for everybody, Debbie.

DEBBIE. No, I should go. Bye, Ex.

EX. See you around, Debbie.

DEBBIE. Yeah. *(Debbie exits.)*

WILLY. Am I wearing the wrong cologne or something?

What'd I say?

EX.   Oh, *man.*

WILLY.   What's going on?

EX.   Get this —

WILLY.   You want a bong hit?

EX.   *Please. (Willy fixes Ex a bong hit.)*

WILLY.   What's going on?

EX.   Get this. I'm at the party —

WILLY.   You weren't at the party. I looked for you.

EX.   Well, I left. If you'd let me finish.

WILLY.   Continue.

EX.   I'm at the party, you know, same old shit. And Debbie starts talking to me. Now, you know what I've always thought about Debbie. Very cute. Too fucking dangerous. Friend of Robin's. Not worth the trouble. But now — now that everything's different. Well. That was then, this is now.

WILLY.   The Outsiders.

EX.   Rumble Fish.

WILLY.   Smoke this, Tex. *(Ex takes a bong hit.)*

EX.   Thanks.

WILLY.   Want a chaser?

EX.   I'm covered. *(They clink the two bottles of Jack Daniels together and each take a slug. Willy fixes another bong hit.)* Anyway, one thing leads to another, we end up coming back here, start fooling around, blah blah blah, she gets panicky, feeling guilty about Robin, all that crap. So I say, fine, if we can't do anything, let's talk about what we'd *like* to do if we *could* do anything. Fantasies, you know. She says she can't tell me hers because then I'd do it. I promise not to. She says her fantasy — get this — her fantasy is for me to take her against her will.

WILLY.   *(Beat.)* You're full of shit.

EX.   Scout's honor.

WILLY.   *Bullshit* Scout.

EX.   I speak the truth.

WILLY.   You mean to tell me you just got laid?

EX.   No, I didn't do it.

WILLY.   What?

EX.   I started to, but she said Stop, so I stopped.

WILLY.   What?

EX.   I stopped.

WILLY.   Why?

EX.   She said Stop.

WILLY.   You *idiot.* That was part of her fantasy.

EX.   She sounded sincere.

WILLY.   Of *course* she did. It's not against her will if you know she wants you to keep going. Against Her Will means *Against Her Will.* You idiot. She was alone with you in your room, on your bed, telling you her fantasy is for you to take her against her will. Read the road map. You should have boned her.

EX.   I didn't feel like it.

WILLY.   *I* did. I could have lived vicariously through you. But no, you had to stop. Why? "She asked me to." What's next, she's going to ask you to carry her books for her? Make her bed? I don't know *what* you were thinking, man. *(Willy takes a bong hit.)*

EX.   There are so many Debbies in this world, you ever notice that?

WILLY.   I don't feel like talking to you. You're a *geek.*

EX.   Interchangeable people. The *Debbies* ...

WILLY.   You're not just like a pencil protector *nerd* geek. You're the kind of geek that bites the heads off of *chickens* ...

EX.   I can't stand the tiniest things. All those Debbies. How this one's voice sounds, what that one talks about, their perfume, their clothes, their souls —

WILLY.   When they don't let you fuck them.

EX.   Is everything about *sex,* Willy?

WILLY.   Yeah.

EX.   I *know.*

WILLY.   *(Beat.)* You should've fucked her.

EX.   You think so?

WILLY.   No question. You could've fulfilled her fantasy. *(Imitates Tattoo on* Fantasy Island.) "De plane, de plane!" Think about it.

EX.   You think she's hot?

WILLY.   Who? Debbie?

EX.   Yeah.

WILLY.   Are you kidding me? She's *very* hot.

EX.   So I fucked up?

WILLY.   Unquestionably. How many more times do I need to say it? But, hey, it's done. Signed, sealed, delivered. Don't dwell. Don't fixate. *Drink. (They clink the bottles of Jack Daniels together and each take a slug. Beat. They clink and drink again. Beat. They clink.)*

EX.   Let's switch bottles.

WILLY.   Why?

EX.   To cut through the tedium.

WILLY.   But they're both J.D ...

EX.   So what's the problem? *(They switch bottles and drink. Beat.)* That's so weird ...

WILLY.   You know ... they taste different ...

EX.   This one's ... sweeter or something ...

WILLY.   How can that be?

EX.   You can't trust brand names anymore, I tell you —

WILLY.   Subtle gradations, fucking everywhere you turn —

EX.   Nothing solid.

WILLY.   99 & 44/100ths percent pure my *ass* —

EX.   Nothing ...

WILLY.   Subtle gradations ...

EX.   I want to kiss somebody.

WILLY.   You just did.

EX.   I want to kiss somebody else.

WILLY.   What are you, The Kissing Bandit? Relax. Do another bong hit.

EX.   I don't want another bong hit.

WILLY.   Have a drink.

EX.   I've already *had* one. I've been drinking all night. I want a kiss. I don't care who, I don't care why, I don't care — I want a *kiss! (Willy grabs Ex and kisses him. They kiss for a few moments, then break from it. Beat.)* You could use a shave, man.

WILLY.   I hate shaving ...

EX.   Stubble's a bitch.

WILLY. Yeah, well …

EX. *(Beat.)* That was weird.

WILLY. I just wanted to shut you up.

EX. Still … that was *weird.*

WILLY. It wasn't *that* weird.

EX. It was *that* weird, Willy.

WILLY. All I did was kiss you.

EX. Oh, that's all?

WILLY. Yeah.

EX. Oh. *(Ex takes a slug of his Jack Daniels.)* Can we switch back? This one's *really* sweet.

WILLY. Here. *(They switch the bottles back and each take a couple of slugs. Silence.)*

EX. I miss Robin. *(Beat.)* When things were good between us … I don't know. She made me feel *smart,* like I was doing something right. *(Beat.)* Oh, *man* … *(Beat.)* Why do we love 'em more when they're gone?

WILLY. I'm not gonna waste my time answering your stupid country music questions …

EX. That was not a country music question. That question had nothing to *do* with country music.

WILLY. Oh, *please. (Imitates Willie Nelson singing.)* "Why do we love 'em … more … when they're gone?" You could be the third *Judd.*

EX. *(Beat.)* Are you worried about graduating?

WILLY. Hell, no. *(Beat.)* A little, I guess. *(Beat.)* I just don't want to ever have to wear *shoes.*

EX. What if I go into the Real World and never see Robin again?

WILLY. You'll see her again. You'll run into her in a supermarket or something. It'll be like that Dan Fogelberg song. I promise.

EX. What song?

WILLY. You know what song.

EX. No, I don't.

WILLY. You know.

EX. *No.*

WILLY.   You know …

EX.   No, I don't.

WILLY.   You know.

EX.   *No.*

WILLY.   You know…. This guy bumps into this chick he used to bone while he's food shopping on New Year's or some shit…. It's *snowing*…. They talk in a car…. It's completely sappy but also kind of cool. You know …

EX.   *Yeah … (Beat.)* I think it's *Christmas* …

WILLY.   It's *totally* New Year's.

EX.   That's Dan Fogelberg?

WILLY.   Who else?

EX.   That's a *good* song.

WILLY.   Makes me *weep*, man. Weep like a fucking *girl.*

BOTH.   *(Beat.)* To Dan Fogelberg. *(They clink their bottles together and drink.)*

EX.   *(Beat.)* To Dan.

WILLY.   To Dan. *(Clink and drink.)*

EX.   *(Beat.)* Fogelberg.

WILLY.   Fogelberg. *(Clink and drink … and drink some more. Long pause.)*

EX.   You're not a bad kisser, man.

WILLY.   Hey, you're no slouch yourself, pal. *(Beat.) To* Dan Fogelberg.

EX.   And your mother.

WILLY.   *Shut up. (Clink and drink.)*

EX.   *(Pause.)* All I have to look forward to in the future is a Dan Fogelberg song? When you think about it, that's kind of really fucking *depressing. (Willy hands the bong to Ex. Ex takes a bong hit. Long pause.)* Give me your shirt.

WILLY.   What?

EX.   I need your shirt.

WILLY.   You have a shirt.

EX.   I need to borrow yours.

WILLY.   What are you gonna do with it?

EX.   Take the bull by the horns.

WILLY.   What bull? What horns? I do not follow.

EX.   You do not have to.

WILLY.   It's my shirt. I have certain inalienable rights.

EX.   It's vitally important, this will not be forgotten, I will take great care of it, what more do you want?

WILLY.   I want to be sixteen years old again.

EX.   I'll see what I can do. *(Willy takes off his shirt and hands it to Ex. Points to his own sneakers.)* Old … *(Grabs a tape from the stereo and puts it in his pocket.)* New … *(Willy's shirt.)* Borrowed … *(His own shirt.)* Blue …

WILLY.   What's the new tape?

EX.   Chili Peppers.

WILLY.   Any good?

EX.   Yeah, it's okay. *(Grabs a bottle of Jack Daniels and exits. He enters a moment later, exchanges his bottle for the other bottle, and exits. Willy goes to the stereo, puts a tape on, then fixes himself another bong hit. He pulls out his squirt gun filled with Cran-Blueberry juice and squirts some into the bong, then takes a bong hit and exhales.)*

WILLY.   Ahh. Happiness is … a Cran-Blueberry bong hit. *(Pause.)* Happiness is … a green and blue round thing called Earth. *(Pause.)* Happiness is … little me in my old brown snowsuit, going down a white hill on my sled, salty wet snot dripping into my smiling mouth, *Mom* waiting inside, making fresh hot chocolate with marshmallows … the glare of the sun on the snow almost blinding me … *(Pause.)* What the hell am I talking about? *(Beat.)* What the hell am I doing in Ex's room … without my *shirt*? *(Beat.)* What the *hell*…?

Scene 6

Robin pours a glass of wine for Debbie. Igor continues to sleep soundly on the bed.

DEBBIE.   I just feel like such a *whorebag*.

ROBIN.   You're not a whorebag … whatever a *whorebag* may be. Here. *(Robin hands Debbie the glass of wine.)*

DEBBIE.   Thanks. *(Takes a sip.)* You would never do this to me, yet there I was, doing it to you —

ROBIN.   You didn't do anything wrong. We're not together. I'm not going to lie to you, yes, I'm annoyed, yes, I'm upset, but I understand it. It's expected by now when it comes to him. It's par for his course.

DEBBIE.   He probably thinks I just *do* this sort of thing … all the time.

ROBIN.   I'm sure he doesn't think that — He rarely ever *thinks* —

DEBBIE.   He *should*. I *do*. I'm a *whorebag*.

ROBIN.   Which is *what*, exactly?

DEBBIE.   Oh, Robin, come on. You know what a whorebag is.

ROBIN.   No, actually, I don't.

DEBBIE.   It's *me*. A whorebag is *me*. *I'm* a whorebag. You're looking at one. *(There is a knock on the door.)*

ROBIN.   Who is it?

EX.   *(Off.)* It's me!

ROBIN.   *Ex*?

EX.   *(Off.)* Yeah.

ROBIN.   What is it, Ex?

EX.   *(Off.)* I need to ask you something.

ROBIN.   Wait a minute! *(To Debbie.)* Sit down, relax, I'll get rid of him.

DEBBIE.   Thanks. *(Debbie sits on the bed. She looks at Igor, then drinks some wine. Robin opens the door. Ex is on his knees in the hall, holding Willy's shirt. He can't see the part of the room where the bed is.)*

ROBIN.   What's up?

EX.   I was wondering ... if you would like ... to get married. *(Beat.)* To me.

ROBIN.   Ex ... what are you talking about?

EX.   Holy matrimony ... Batman ... I mean Robin. *(Beat.)* I'm proposing ... to you. As tradition dictates, I am on my knees. *(Beat.)* Like George Washington never actually said, I cannot tell a lie. I do not come bearing an engagement ring.... In lieu of such.... However.... Please accept this shirt. As a symbol. Of my desire. To be committed to you. For the rest of ... my life. *(Beat.)* It's only a symbol. You can't actually keep it. It's Willy's shirt. See the ring-around-the-collar? That's not just ordinary ring-around-the-collar, that's *engagement* ring-around-the-collar. *(Beat.)* If you choose to accept my aforementioned offer, of course, you can redeem the shirt for a sizable engagement ring, to be followed by a wedding band.

ROBIN.   I smell alcohol on your breath ...

EX.   I did a few shots of Jack Daniels before I came over ... so I wouldn't smell like mouthwash.

ROBIN.   Ex, I think maybe you should go back to your room and get some sleep —

EX.   I may have had a drink or two, but I am in complete control of my faculties and what's more, I want you to be my betrothed. What do you say? Huh?

ROBIN.   What led you, after all this time, to suddenly come here and ask me to marry you?

EX.   I had this flash. I feel so alone most of the time — you know, all these gaps everywhere — everything's all broken-up — you and me, my band, pretty soon school will be over and what's left? More of the same. Right? I admit, I've been stupid. *(Robin looks down at Ex, who's looking up at her. She shakes her head.)*

ROBIN.   You're such a little boy. You're this cute, messy little boy who's always getting into trouble.

EX.   Forgive me. For all the bad things I've ever done. Love me again, like you used to. Love me like that. Save me from this parade of meaningless encounters. I'm just going through the motions, Robin. But you and I — we were great together. At our peak. We were something to see.

ROBIN.   You really should get some rest, Ex.

EX.   Can I come in?

ROBIN.   I don't think that's a very good idea —

EX.   Come on —

ROBIN.   I don't think that's a very good idea *at all* ...

EX.   Why not?

ROBIN.   Well — *(Debbie gets up and starts to walk out.)*

DEBBIE.   I've gotta go, Robin, I'll see you later.

ROBIN.   Debbie, don't go —

DEBBIE.   Bye. *(Debbie exits.)*

EX.   *(Beat.)* Bye! *(Beat.)* What was she doing here?

ROBIN.   She just needed someone to talk to. She had a rough night.

EX.   Oh. *(Beat.)* What ... *sort of* rough night?

ROBIN.   I think you know.

EX.   She told you?

ROBIN.   Yeah.

EX.   *Fuck. (Beat.)* What ever happened to fucking *discretion,* you know? Whatever happened to fucking *trust? No trust! No discretion! Fucking emotional anarchy!*

ROBIN.   Stop yelling!

EX.   Will you marry me?

ROBIN.   Are you out of your mind?

EX.   I'm dead serious.

ROBIN.   You *attacked* Debbie an hour ago and now you want me to seriously consider your marriage proposal?

EX.   Yeah.

ROBIN.   *(Beat.)* No, Ex, I will not marry you.

EX.   *(Beat.)* You know what your problem is, Robin? Huh? Do you?

ROBIN.   I have a feeling I'm about to find out.

EX.   You make these meaningless little distinctions into things of importance. So *what* if Debbie and I fooled around tonight? So *what?* In a way, that's what made me realize I needed something more permanent in my life. And that something is *you,* Robin.

ROBIN.   No, it's not.

EX.   *(Beat.)* Your problem is, you care about the difference between "who" and "whom" and guess what, Robin? There *is* no difference. It doesn't *matter*. It's not *important*. Nobody cares about these things but *you*.

ROBIN. You drink too much.

EX. You don't drink enough. *(Jack suddenly walks past Ex in the hallway. They look at each other for a moment.)*

JACK. Hey.

EX. Hey. *(Jack continues walking and is gone. Robin is startled and looks at Jack walking away. Ex grabs his bottle of Jack Daniels, which has been out of sight in the hallway, and starts to walk into the room. Robin's attention returns to Ex.)*

ROBIN. What are you doing?

EX. I want to show you something.

ROBIN. I don't think —

EX. I just want to show you something. *(Ex walks over to the goldfish bowl, reaches in, takes out the fish, swallows it, and washes it down with a slug of Jack Daniels.)* I always wanted to do that. Swallow a goldfish. Very collegiate.

ROBIN. That was *Anastasia!*

EX. She was just a fish.

ROBIN. She was *Anastasia!*

EX. She was just a fish with a long Russian name, don't get all sentimental and — *(Sees Igor sleeping on the bed.)* Hey. *(Walks over to Igor and wakes him up.)* Hey. What the hell are you doing?

IGOR. What...?

ROBIN. Ex —

EX. You're good. You're smooth. Stabbed me in the back and I didn't even notice.

IGOR. What are you *talking* about?

EX. What do you *think* I'm talking about? Whose bed is this?

IGOR. Hmm...?

EX. I could fucking *kill* you —

IGOR. You think I —

ROBIN. Ex, nothing happened here —

EX. I *should* fucking kill you —

ROBIN. Not that it would be any of your business if —

51

EX.   How dare you? I've been *inside* her. How *dare* you?

IGOR.   I came here to tell her —

EX.   You *disgust* me. You're a pathetic little back-stabbing, deceitful motherfucking thief. You stole what was mine.

IGOR.   *(Beat.)* Sorry ...

EX.   You *should* be.

IGOR.   For you. I mean I'm sorry for *you. (To Robin.)* Do you want me to stick around?

ROBIN.   No, that's okay, Igor. Ex isn't staying.

IGOR.   See you around, Robin.

ROBIN.   Thanks for stopping by. *(Igor exits.)*

EX.   *(Beat.)* I'd like an explanation.

ROBIN.   You would be astonishingly funny if you weren't so goddamn *sad.*

EX.   I *mean* it. I would like an explanation.

ROBIN.   Yeah, well, I'd like Anastasia back. Too bad, huh?

EX.   What was he doing here?

ROBIN.   Trying to give me a scoop. Unfortunately, we're not putting out any more issues before graduation. But his intentions were as honorable as could be. He was just trying to give me a scoop about *Whitey.* Remember Whitey?

EX.   Yeah, I remember Whitey.

ROBIN.   At least you haven't forgotten everything.

EX.   I remember Whitey, and I don't *give* a fuck about Whitey, I just asked you to *marry* me —

ROBIN.   And I said no, and you're probably going to have one whopper of a headache tomorrow morning. Good night.

EX.   Robin —

ROBIN.   *Good-Night.*

EX.   We had our good times ...

ROBIN.   And our bad times.

EX.   I'll be fine.

ROBIN.   Glad to hear it.

EX.   I don't need you.

ROBIN.   Good to know. Good night. *(Ex is in the hallway now. Robin shuts the door and locks it.)*

EX.   *(Off.) Fucking bitch!* (Ex pounds on the door. Robin walks over to the empty fishbowl and stares at it for a moment or two, then *pours the remaining wine from the bottle into the fishbowl, turning the water maroon. Off.) Come out here! I'm not finished talking! Come out here right now! I'm not finished! I'm ... not ... finished! (Ex continues pounding on the door as Robin stares at the fishbowl full of watered-down red wine, her arms crossed in front of her.)*

Scene 7

Whitey is sitting on a metal folding chair, drinking a cup of coffee.

WHITEY.   Hello, my name is Whitey, and I'm an alcoholic.
ALL.   HI, WHITEY!
WHITEY.   *Hi ... (Sips some coffee.)* Somewhere, there's a room filled with coffee addicts drinking bourbon out of cardboard cups, telling caffeine horror stories, I just know it. *(Beat.)* Umm, I've been sober now for a hundred and fifty days, and it's still ... it's still very difficult, which shouldn't come as a surprise to anybody here. I lost my job and at that time, when I needed clarity more than ever, I turned to booze instead. *(Beat.) Booze.* I like saying "booze" more than *alcohol* or *liquor* ... or *spirits. (Beat.) Booze.* It just sounds *right. (Beat.)* Anyhow, I was a fantastic rationalizer. I got into the habit of quoting *Keats* — to others, to myself, it didn't matter.

> Give me Women, Wine, and Snuff
> Until I cry out, 'Hold, enough!'
> You may do so sans objection
> Till the day of resurrection;
> For, bless my beard, they aye shall be
> My beloved Trinity.

Damn fine poem. Even better with some whiskey sloshing around inside you. *(Beat.)* A college campus is one of the best places to cultivate and sustain a drinking problem. I'd swear there were usually more drunks at one of our college faculty meetings than there are in this room right now. Suffice to say, I would start drinking, and ... well, I *drank*. And *drank*. Taught classes I don't remember teaching because I was so tanked up, so *loaded.* Things certainly don't get easier as we get older. *(Beat.)* I was a very pretty child. *(Pause.)* On his way to dying — a bit before he died — my great-grandfather cracked a bit, fell a touch insane and claimed to be — actually, *insisted* he was God. Demanded we call him God. Wouldn't answer to anything *but* "God." Ever since, when I hear the word "God," what first comes to mind is this image of a mad old inconti-nent Irish relative. *(Beat.)* So a few of the Twelve Steps were tough for me at first, since God as I understood Him was my great-grandfather. *(Beat.)* At the beginning, the pressure my *lawyers* put upon me to get sober was a big part of it. They forced me to admit to myself that, yes, I was an alcoholic. I *am* an alcoholic. I had to set aside more than just the booze. I had to set aside my ego, my *pride,* my instinct to talk down to people, to *teach.* But now, I admit it willingly. I'm a *grate-ful* alcoholic, with five months of sobriety behind me. *(Beat.)* I've heard that if a person forces a smile long enough, chances are good that person will end up *happy.*

Scene 8

Pomp & Circumstance *plays. Robin enters and stands in front of a microphone.*

ROBIN.   When I was a little girl, I was so *confident* and *certain,* daydreaming in my suburban Illinois bedroom, all nice and safe and clean and frilly. My parents, who are here right now — wave to the crowd, folks. *(Points.)* That's them. They used to make me settle fights with my playmates. They'd call them *de-bates,* but don't let that fool you. They were fights. *(Beat.)* This school's administrators recently paid an enormous sum of money to *settle.* To keep a former professor from taking them to court to challenge a decision *they* made. This doesn't feel like a fight, or a debate — not really. This feels like compromise. This feels

... very *Hollow.* What is this supposed to mean to us, as we're about to graduate from this place, with diplomas from an institution that's telling us to settle? *(Beat.)* I know that eventually, when understanding runs out, there is a need for judgment, but *who* is qualified to judge? And who is qualified to *judge* who is qualified to judge? Who picks the judges? Who decides that it's okay — to settle? *(Beat.)* Everybody in my hometown was shocked when I chose this place, but they shouldn't have been. Martha Graham danced here. I used to envision myself — secretly, of course — as the heir apparent to Martha Graham. Here was a *woman* making exotic *shapes* — her shapes made more powerful statements than all the tainted rhetoric in the air. *(Beat.)* If I could only *dance* all of this ... *(Pause.)* But ... I can't. *(Beat.)* I've tried to find some truth during my time here, some *wisdom,* beyond food and sleep and sex and *showers.* What's worth giving to? I don't know. I wish I did. *(Beat.)* I suppose *settling* can also mean coming to some sort of peace, and I do hope we all find some sort of peace in our lives.... *All* of us. Anybody ... anybody who's ever been in pain. And whether *we* settle or ... *not* ... remains to be seen.

END OF PLAY

PROPERTY LIST

ACT ONE

Envelope (IGOR)
School newspaper (IGOR, EX)
Guitar (EX)
Teapot with tea (WHITEY)
Tea cups with tea (or mugs) (WHITEY)
Vodka (WHITEY)
Vodka shot glass (WHITEY)
Typewriter (ROBIN)
Beers (WILLY, EX)
Tape recorder (ROBIN)
Christmas lights on string (EX, IGOR)
Small liquor bottle (WHITEY)

ACT TWO

Small portable TV
Plastic toy gun with rubber darts (EX)
Cran-blueberry juice in bottle (WILLY)
Squirt gun (WILLY)
Sesame noodles in white Chinese take-out container (IGOR)
Fork or chopsticks (IGOR)
Goldfish in bowl (DEBBIE)
Pad of paper (ROBIN)
Bottle of wine (ROBIN)
Glasses for wine (ROBIN, DEBBIE, IGOR)
Bottle of Jack Daniels whiskey (EX, WILLY)
Bong (WILLY)
Cassette tapes (EX, WILLY)
Cup of coffee (WHITEY)

NOTE ON THE SET

I thought Allen Moyer's set for the first production of SOPH-ISTRY was wonderfully simple: A neutral, cream-colored up-stage wall with two doors, one on the far left, the other on the far right. In between these was a lightly imposing wooden desk, with a swiveling wooden desk chair between the desk and the wall. There were two beds, one stage right (Ex's room or Whitey's apartment), the other stage left (Robin's room), each with a bookshelf on the side that was closest to the respective wall. At the front of the stage was a small ledge that charac-ters could sit on, and under which various props could be stored, unseen by the audience until brought into play. This setting suggested the play's conflicts (opposing beds and doors, with the desk judging from the center) and evoked a college campus, allowing for settings both specific (Ex and Robin's dorm rooms, Quintana's office, Whitey's classroom and apart-ment) and general (party, shopping mall, A.A. meeting, gradu-ation) and, most importantly, allowing the play to move and flow instead of forcing it to grind to a halt for clunky transi-tions.

NEW PLAYS

• **MERE MORTALS** by David Ives, author of *All in the Timing*. Another critically acclaimed evening of one-act comedies combining wit, satire, hilarity and intellect -- a winning combination. The entire evening of plays can be performed by 3 men and 3 women. ISBN: 0-8222-1632-9

• **BALLAD OF YACHIYO** by Philip Kan Gotanda. A provocative play about innocence, passion and betrayal, set against the backdrop of a Hawaiian sugar plantation in the early 1900s. *"Gotanda's writing is superb ... a great deal of fine craftsmanship on display here, and much to enjoy."* --*Variety*. *"...one of the country's most consistently intriguing playwrights..."* --*San Francisco Examiner*. *"As he has in past plays, Gotanda defies expectations..."* --*Oakland Tribune*. [3M, 4W] ISBN: 0-8222-1547-0

• **MINUTES FROM THE BLUE ROUTE** by Tom Donaghy. While packing up a house, a family converges for a weekend of flaring tempers and shattered illusions. *"With MINUTES FROM THE BLUE ROUTE [Donaghy] succeeds not only in telling a story -- a typically American one with wide appeal, about how parents and kids struggle to understand each other and mostly fail -- but in notating it inventively, through wittily elliptical, crisscrossed speeches, and in making it carry a fairly vast amount of serious weight with surprising ease."* --*Village Voice*. [2M, 2W] ISBN: 0-8222-1608-6

• **SCAPIN** by Molière, adapted by Bill Irwin and Mark O'Donnell. This adaptation of Molière's 325-year-old farce, *Les Fourberies de Scapin*, keeps the play in period while adding a late Twentieth Century spin to the language and action. *"This SCAPIN, [with a] felicitous adaptation by Mark O'Donnell, would probably have gone over big with the same audience who first saw Molière's Fourberies de Scapin...in Paris in 1671."* --*N.Y. Times*. *"Commedia dell'arte and vaudeville have at least two things in common: baggy pants and Bill Irwin. All make for a natural fit in the celebrated clown's entirely unconventional adaptation."* --*Variety* [9M, 3W, flexible] ISBN: 0-8222-1603-5

• **THE TURN OF THE SCREW** adapted for the stage by Jeffrey Hatcher from the story by Henry James. The American master's classic tale of possession is given its most interesting "turn" yet: one woman plays the mansion's terrified governess while a single male actor plays everyone else. *"In his thoughtful adaptation of Henry James' spooky tale, Jeffrey Hatcher does away with the supernatural flummery, exchanging the story's balanced ambiguities about the nature of reality for a portrait of psychological vampirism..."* --*Boston Globe*. [1M, 1W] ISBN: 0-8222-1554-3

• **NEVILLE'S ISLAND** by Tim Firth. A middle management orientation exercise turns into an hilarious disaster when the team gets "shipwrecked" on an uninhabited island. *"NEVILLE'S ISLAND ... is that rare event: a genuinely good new play..., it's a comedic, adult LORD OF THE FLIES..."* --*The Guardian*. *"... A non-stop, whitewater deluge of comedy both sophisticated and slapstick.... Firth takes a perfect premise and shoots it to the extreme, flipping his fish out of water, watching them flop around a bit, and then masterminding the inevitable feeding frenzy."* --*New Mexican*. [4M] ISBN: 0-8222-1581-0

DRAMATISTS PLAY SERVICE, INC.
440 Park Avenue South, New York, NY 10016 212-683-8960 Fax 212-213-1539
postmaster@dramatists.com www.dramatists.com

NEW PLAYS

• **TAKING SIDES by Ronald Harwood.** Based on the true story of one of the world's greatest conductors whose wartime decision to remain in Germany brought him under the scrutiny of a U.S. Army determined to prove him a Nazi. *"A brave, wise and deeply moving play delineating the confrontation between culture, and power, between art and politics, between irresponsible freedom and responsible compromise." --London Sunday Times.* [4M, 3W] ISBN: 0-8222-1566-7

• **MISSING/KISSING by John Patrick Shanley.** Two biting short comedies, MISSING MARISA and KISSING CHRISTINE, by one of America's foremost dramatists and the Academy Award winning author of *Moonstruck.* *" ... Shanley has an unusual talent for situations ... and a sure gift for a kind of inner dialogue in which people talk their hearts as well as their minds...." --N.Y. Post.* MISSING MARISA [2M], KISSING CHRISTINE [1M, 2W] ISBN: 0-8222-1590-X

• **THE SISTERS ROSENSWEIG by Wendy Wasserstein, Pulitzer Prize-winning author of** *The Heidi Chronicles.* Winner of the 1993 Outer Critics Circle Award for Best Broadway Play. A captivating portrait of three disparate sisters reuniting after a lengthy separation on the eldest's 50th birthday. *"The laughter is all but continuous." --New Yorker.* *"Funny. Observant. A play with wit as well as acumen.... In dealing with social and cultural paradoxes, Ms. Wasserstein is, as always, the most astute of commentators." --N.Y. Times.* [4M, 4W] ISBN: 0-8222-1348-6

• **MASTER CLASS by Terrence McNally. Winner of the 1996 Tony Award for Best Play.** Only a year after winning the Tony Award for *Love! Valour! Compassion!,* Terrence McNally scores again with the most celebrated play of the year, an unforgettable portrait of Maria Callas, our century's greatest opera diva. *"One of the white-hot moments of contemporary theatre. A total triumph." --N.Y. Post. "Blazingly theatrical." -- USA Today.* [3M, 3W] ISBN: 0-8222-1521-7

• **DEALER'S CHOICE by Patrick Marber.** A weekly poker game pits a son addicted to gambling against his own father, who also has a problem but won't admit it. *"... make tracks to DEALER'S CHOICE, Patrick Marber's wonderfully masculine, razor-sharp dissection of poker-as-life.... It's a play that comes out swinging and never lets up -- a witty, wisecracking drama that relentlessly probes the tortured souls of its six very distinctive ... characters. CHOICE is a cutthroat pleasure that you won't want to miss." --Time Out (New York).* [6M] ISBN: 0-8222-1616-7

• **RIFF RAFF by Laurence Fishburne.** RIFF RAFF marks the playwriting debut of one of Hollywood's most exciting and versatile actors. *"Mr. Fishburne is surprisingly and effectively understated, with scalding bubbles of anxiety breaking through the surface of a numbed calm." --N.Y. Times. "Fishburne has a talent and a quality...[he] possesses one of the vital requirements of a playwright -- a good ear for the things people say and the way they say them." --N.Y. Post.* [3M] ISBN: 0-8222-1545-4

DRAMATISTS PLAY SERVICE, INC.
440 Park Avenue South, New York, NY 10016 212-683-8960 Fax 212-213-1539
postmaster@dramatists.com www.dramatists.com